Receiving God's Mercy

by

Mirek Hufton

Receiving God's Mercy
ISBN 0-88144-288-3
Copyright © 2006 by
Mirek Hufton
320 Hardscrabble Road
Roswell, GA 30075

Published by
Christian Publishing Services
P. O. Box 701434
Tulsa, OK 74170

Cover Design: Bobby Simpson
Text Design: Lisa Simpson

Dedication

To my one and only, my wife Linda, who stood by and supported me through one of the greatest trials in my life and who believed with me for the victory which I received.

Acknowledgments

I would like to acknowledge and thank my wife, Linda, for her encouragement, Theresa Gardner for an outstanding job on editing, Julie Loehr for designing the cover and finally, a dear friend, Billy Godwin, who gave me the inspiration to begin.

Contents

Introduction

Receiving God's Mercy

In 1994 I was diagnosed with advanced Hodgkin's disease. I was given just ninety days to live. This book is the story of my deliverance from cancer, but it's also a lot more than that. Woven into the story is my fresh discovery of God's great mercy. That may seem like an odd statement coming from a minister, but trust me, it's not.

What is mercy? If you look it up in the dictionary, it says things like "the feeling that motivates compassion." Actually, I hate that definition. If mercy is a feeling, then it's fleeting. It may or may not be available at any given point in time. When a criminal is on trial, he might "throw himself on the mercy of the court." Good luck with that! In the old western movies, the bad guy would always have to "beg for mercy" before he had to "reach for the sky." You never wanted to be the guy who had to "beg for mercy" in one of those movies. Why? Because no mercy was going to be shown! And the few times when mercy was granted, it always made the recipient seem pathetic.

I'm telling you that mercy isn't a feeling God has that comes and goes depending on the circumstances. It's part of His nature. And it's something for which every human being is desperately in need! There's nothing pitiful or sad about needing mercy. We all need it!

This book is for people who are going through the battle of their lives. I pray that the things I learned in the struggle of my life will fuel you for victory in your fight. No matter what you face – disease, divorce, financial ruin – you are not alone. In this book, you won't find a finger pointed at a failing parent, a four-step solution to your problem, or any kind of personal accusation for why you're dealing with challenging issues. I've got much better news!

Maybe you're like me. You've studied a lot of the Bible and faith-filled writings. You're ready with answers to theological questions. When you need something, you know all the right ways to approach God. Or maybe you're living at the other end of the spectrum. Maybe you've always thought of God as a strict disciplinarian and you're afraid to approach Him at all. Maybe you go to church and look around at everyone else wondering how they have it all together. But at both ends of that spectrum, there's a key element missing – God's mercy. We don't talk or study much about mercy, which is ironic considering how desperately we need it!

I wrote my story to bring hope to those who find themselves in circumstances similar to mine, or those who are going through other kinds of life-challenging trials. By God's grace, may you find fresh hope, strong faith, and determined purpose to receive a miracle from heaven.

Mirek Hufton

"*I came that they [you] may have and enjoy life, and have it in abundance (to the full, till it overflows).*"

John 10:10 AMP

1

Life Is for Living

"All of your hair will fall out with this treatment."

I was looking straight into the doctor's eyes, but it felt as though I was listening to him from under water. He gave me a thick notebook detailing all of the side effects of this particular type of chemotherapy. He gently and thoroughly explained what his patients usually go through. I listened to every word. This doctor was a highly respected physician, holding a Ph.D. in Philosophy in addition to his M.D. in Oncology. He encouraged me with the news that he'd had a great deal of success in fighting my particular form of cancer.

Cancer. What an ugly word. But it was one I had grown used to hearing. My wife Linda was an oncology nurse. Her daily conversation was filled with stories of cancer-related tragedy and triumph. But her stories had been nothing more to me than casual conversation, a loving spouse telling the tales of her workday. After my diagnosis, her experience, understanding, and faith became invaluable.

It was totally surreal to me that I would be diagnosed with a terminal condition. That kind of thing just didn't happen to me. My entire life, I'd always been healthy and strong, sucking the marrow out of life and living on the edge. My parents were missionaries and they raised my brothers and me in South Africa. The African landscape is wild and untamed, possessing a beauty that defies description. The mountains jut out of the valleys right through the clouds. They reach up for something and nothing can stand in their way. The open vistas there are like those up in the big sky country of Montana, but even more breathtaking.

When you go somewhere in rural Africa, you don't just go on a whim. You have to be ready to fight your way through. Our family didn't drive a car. We had a Land Rover Defender. Right now you're probably thinking of the soccer-mom version with dual heated seats and air-conditioning. It wasn't that kind of Land Rover. This was a vehicle with teeth! It ate up the African dirt roads – or the lack thereof – and got us where we needed to go!

When there was a river that we had to cross, there was no fancy suspension bridge to get us over. In fact, at times there were no bridges at all because rivers would often swell to flood stage and swallow the bridges. When we couldn't see the bridges, did that mean we stayed on our side and waited for the water to recede? No! Many times the bridges that had no sides to them would be completely submerged under water without any trace of a bridge being there at all. My father would simply jump out of the Land Rover, disconnect the fan belt (so the water would not splash on the electrical system and short it out) and get right back in the driver's side. We would cross that river slowly – mother, father, and kids riding through water completely submerging all four tires and sometimes even coming up to the doors.

As a young child, I lived in what was my idea of "Six Flags." My childhood in Africa was filled with the sort of daily adventures that any boy would love. I recall a time as a young boy living with our family in a thatch cottage by ourselves surrounded by the open African veldt. One day the three-foot dry grass caught fire some distance away and was spreading across the entire horizon. Since the wind was blowing strongly in our direction, the fire was approaching rapidly. I remember as a young boy wondering how in the world we would escape total destruction.

When there is a fire in Africa, you don't dial 911. I remember my father racing off and gathering all the village people around for help. They knew exactly what to do. Each one quickly cut down a large branch from local trees and ran towards the fire. I recall dozens of faithful villagers spread out in long lines who literally were beating out the fire a hundred feet or so from our thatch cottage. It was a close one. There was always something interesting and exciting happening in Africa.

After about thirteen years of mission work, our family moved to the United States. We moved to Chicago, Illinois, which felt like I had gone to another planet. It took some getting used to. To be honest, throughout my teen years, I was always on a quest to move back to Africa.

Things changed for me in college. It was in my college years that I had a personal encounter with God and my passion for Africa was surpassed by my zeal for God. Of course, I'd been raised as the son of missionaries, so I had always believed in God and attended church. But in college, He got a firm hold of my heart, filled me with His Spirit, and put His power within me!

My concept of God and Christianity went from pious religious understanding to total being, raw passion, and divine relationship. It's like the difference between having a crush on someone and being married. After I experienced the infilling of the Holy Spirit, I also discovered that God would heal a sick person if he simply asked in faith! Let me tell you how I came to that conclusion.

"I am the Lord who heals you."

"Surely He has borne our griefs (sicknesses, weaknesses, and diseases) and carried our sorrows and pains [of punishment], yet we [ignorantly] considered Him stricken, smitten, and afflicted by God [as if with leprosy].

"But He was wounded for our transgressions, He was bruised for our guilt and iniquities; the chastisement [needful to obtain] peace and well-being for us was upon Him, and with the stripes [that wounded] Him we are healed and made whole."

Isaiah 53:4-5 AMP

2

God's a Healer

As you read the Gospels according to Matthew, Mark, Luke, and John, you see Jesus traveling from town to town teaching, preaching, and healing. Jesus specifically attributed the cause of the sickness and its effects to the work of Satan, either directly or indirectly. I began to see clearly that all sickness and disease is an attack on the human body to bring dis-ease, dis-comfort, pain, suffering, and eventually death.

The famous physician, Luke, in the Gospel summarized Jesus' ministry as follows: **"How God anointed Jesus of Nazareth with the Holy Spirit and power, and how he went around doing good and healing all who were under the power of the devil, because God was with him."**[1]

In a nutshell, what did Jesus do? **"He went around doing good and healing all who were under the power of the devil. . . ."** It says that He did "good." What good did He do? He went about **"HEALING ALL WHO WERE UNDER THE POWER OF THE DEVIL."** And why did He go about doing that good? **"Because God was with him."**

According to the Bible, Jesus **"is the same yesterday, today, and forever."**[2] If that is true (and we know it is), then one of Jesus' primary ministries – bringing healing to the sick and suffering – is as important to Him today as it was then.

I became totally convinced that if we would simply ask God in childlike faith, trusting and believing in His Word, that any one of us could be healed. I've always believed that God would use

15

doctors to help people, but this new realization was about God's miraculous power to bring healing supernaturally.

Doctors are wonderful blessings from God to man. I thank God for all the things they do to alleviate pain and suffering. But doctors are human and they are limited in what they can do. God is supernatural. He performs miracles.

As I studied these scriptures, I began putting them into practice. In my college dorm room, my Christian friends and I began praying for sick people. They would often receive healing right on the spot or within a few days. My faith for healing began to grow. The more I read and studied the Bible and the more I prayed for the sick, the more healings I witnessed. I knew I had discovered a gold mine of truth!

The first personal experience I had with praying for healing was when I discovered that I had impacted wisdom teeth. The dentist showed me the X-rays and he was going to schedule surgery. Shortly thereafter, I was in a church service where a young man stood up and testified that his wisdom teeth had been impacted and he asked God to heal them.

During praise and worship in the service before, he felt the power of God come upon him. Later, he discovered, to his delight, that the Lord had immediately and perfectly straightened out all of his teeth. It was a miracle!

When I heard that testimony, I decided to lay hold of this promise for myself since I suffered from the same ailment. I went about daily life, continuing to study God's Word and believing Him to heal me.

Several months later, I was standing at the mirror brushing my teeth when I noticed that my impacted wisdom teeth were perfectly upright and in proper alignment in my mouth. I said to myself, "Wow! This really does work!" And work it did!

I became increasingly involved in lay ministry, and I had plenty of opportunities to share God's Word of healing and pray for the sick. There were times when nothing seemed to happen, but then there were many times when miracles took place. Once, during a home Bible study, a woman came for prayer who had just returned from Mayo Clinic. She had cancer throughout her body and doctors had told her she had six months – at the longest – to live. We prayed for her. We all really sensed God's power going into her. We rebuked the cancer in Jesus' name and asked the Father to heal her.

Within a week, she was feeling totally fit. She checked with the doctors and they found that the cancer had disappeared completely! Two years later I saw that lady sharing her testimony on a Christian television program. After two years, she was still completely healed and she continued to give all the glory to God for her miracle.

When I talk about healing, I'm not talking about something someone told me or something I saw on television. I have personally seen blind eyes miraculously opened! I've been up close and personal when the deaf and dumb have been healed instantly – hearing and speaking perfectly. I've seen cripples get up to walk and run. I know that I know that God loves His people and He wants to see them well!

My point in sharing these experiences is to explain how God had established my faith for healing over the years. I came to see clearly what God's Word said regarding His healing power and I personally experienced the results. God's healing was no longer a theory to me. It was a reality. It was a fact with simple principles:

1. Healing is always God's will.

2. Healing is an inheritance from God that belongs to us.

3. Sickness is from hell not heaven.

4. It is not God's will that we suffer in sickness and in pain.

5.   Healing is for everyone who asks for it in faith.

After college, I went into my young professional life continuing to work in lay ministry and pray for the sick. I was so busy in ministry and career that I just about forgot to get married! In my early thirties, I thought I'd better get serious with God about getting a wife. I married a beautiful young woman named Linda who was everything I'd ever hoped for in a wife. She was a nurse and an accomplished musician who led worship at church. Her heart beat for God just as passionately as mine.

Over the years, life just kept getting better. We had three healthy, terrific kids. My career in corporate sales was successful. I kept getting promotions, raises, and bonuses. Those were great days.

"Trust in the Lord with all your heart, and lean not on your own understanding;

"In all your ways acknowledge Him, and He shall direct your paths."

Proverbs 3:5-6

3

The Surprise of My Life

Although I loved my work and my career was steadily progressing upward, and my family life I thoroughly enjoyed and life was good, all of a sudden it wasn't good enough anymore. There was something inside of me that said I needed to move on. Even though things were going great in the natural, there was something within me that said I needed to let go of what I was doing for something else.

This was the finger of God on my life. For nearly a year I felt that God was leading me to leave the business world and move into full-time ministry. It was a struggle for me because I really didn't want to do that. I wanted God to find somebody else!

For an entire year, the Lord kept dealing with me and I couldn't shake it. I set a lunch meeting with my pastor at that time, Dr. Bob Wright. My wife and I both respected and loved our pastor as a man who taught God's Word with authority and moved in the supernatural gifts of God.

"Pastor," I said with trepidation, "I keep feeling like there's something more out there for me. I think I'm sensing the Holy Spirit tugging at my heart to go into full-time ministry."

The pastor didn't mince words. "Mirek, if there is any way that you can keep your full-time job, do that. You have to really know you're called to be in ministry. So many people think they're called, but they are better off holding down a good job and working in the Helps Ministry in their church."

I went away from that meeting feeling better about where I was in life. What the pastor said made sense to me, so I jumped back into my business world. However, the urge to enter ministry wouldn't go away.

Several months passed, so I scheduled another lunch meeting with my pastor. I said, "Pastor, I still feel the pull that God wants to use me in full-time ministry. This sense just won't leave me. What do you think about this?"

"Like I said before," he said, "you need to be doing the work of your business. This is just as honorable as doing work in the ministry. You need to support your family and just work with God and work for Him in your free time." Again, I walked away thinking that was right and I went about my business.

But again, over the months, not only did the thoughts not leave me, but they became more intense. It truly became like a fire within me to do the will of God for my life, even if it meant full-time ministry. I came to understand what the prophet Jeremiah said, **"His word was in my heart like a burning fire shut up in my bones; I was weary of holding it back, and I could not."**[3]

So I scheduled one more lunch with my pastor. I said with a strong voice of conviction, "I've come to the place that I don't care if my family has to live under a bridge in a cardboard box. I will live with them and protect them, but I have to serve God full time in the ministry."

I was amazed at his reply. He said, "I think you're ready now!" The past year had been spent in seeking God about this change of careers. Through the pastor's encouragement and my own seeking and waiting on God, I felt the time had come to resign.

When I brought this to the president of the company, he was really upset. He said, "Are you crazy?! You've got a great income. Business is exploding. Are you crazy? Just do this 'God thing' on the weekends."

But I wouldn't be deterred. I resigned anyway. I knew what God had put on my heart, so I stepped out in faith. My wife and I began our ministry together on staff in our local church. Although our income had dropped from a very large figure down to a very small figure, God supplied all of our needs and we thoroughly enjoyed our new life in serving in that great church.

After over six years of faithfully serving in our local church, the Senior Pastor came and offered me his position because he was feeling called to go into the evangelistic field. It was really quite an honor; however, we sensed in our hearts that God was calling us to pioneer a new church in Roswell, Georgia. Because of this strong leading, we left to do that, along with the pastor's blessing.

Starting a church from scratch is not an easy job. We faced enormous challenges, but we felt strongly called to our task and we pushed through the barriers. God's favor was really on our work. Three years later, the church was growing and we were very excited at all the things God was doing in us and through us. Our children were healthy and happy at ages eight, six, and four. I knew that I was working according to God's plan for my life. Things were going great.

It was around that time that I started to get an annoying cough. At first I thought it was allergies or something, but it was persistent. I didn't really think anything about it, but Linda said she didn't like the sound of that cough. She wanted me to get it checked out. I planned to, but I wasn't in any hurry. For weeks I continued coughing.

One weekend I was going out of town to a conference, so I thought I'd pop into the clinic where Linda worked and get a prescription for some antibiotics to wipe out whatever infection I thought I had. I was tired of the continual coughing. In no way, however, was I prepared for the doctor's diagnosis.

During the initial examination, they noticed one of the lymph glands on my neck was swollen. I had noticed it several weeks before but had thought nothing of it. The doctors sent me for an X-ray of my neck and chest.

When the results came back, they couldn't see anything. The film was just solid white. They figured that something was wrong with the machine, so they sent me back for another round. Again, all they saw was a white mass covering my entire chest cavity.

Linda was upset, but she wasn't shocked. That morning she had tried to listen to my lungs with a stethoscope. She had me take several deep breaths, but she heard nothing. She didn't tell me that day. I found out about that a while later. When I was with the physician's assistant, she had also tried to listen to my heart and lungs. Linda watched the puzzled look on the assistant's face and her heart sank.

I have always been a very healthy individual with plenty of energy. I was physically fit and felt strong. My weight was right and I slept well. It was the furthest thing from my mind that I'd ever be attacked with such a deadly disease. To say the least, I was in complete shock. I felt like I was trapped in a nightmare.

"Mirek, we are sorry to report this to you, but you have a large tumor totally enveloping your heart and lungs. We suspect that it's cancer."

The doctor looked at me with deep concern as he spoke those words to me. He was a good friend of my wife. He worked with her and the other nurses every day at Atlanta Cancer Care. And now the dreaded "C" word was given to me. Who, me? Cancer? No way! The doctors kept staring at me with somber expressions that unsettled me greatly.

The doctors immediately sent me to get a CT scan so they could get a more thorough picture of what they were dealing with. As I sat waiting for the technicians to do their tests, my mind whirled. How did this happen? Why me? Why now? Where are You, God? Yet I knew He was with me.

As I reflected on the seriousness of my condition, my mind flashed back over my life. I sat there all alone in the waiting room, contemplating the fact that my body had been taken over by a deadly disease. I literally faced the prospect of leaving this world. I was brought to a fresh realization of how totally dependent I am on the Father for every breath.

It was at this moment when God's comfort from the Scriptures began to embrace me. Hadn't He said that He would never leave me or forsake me? I sensed His reassuring presence. I began to talk with Him, and His peace came to me, settling my heart.

After the scan, my wife and I were ushered into one of the examining rooms with Dr. Tom. He began to explain to me that I had a tumor that had grown throughout my chest cavity, wrapping around my heart and lungs. It had started to choke off my bronchial tubes, which is why I'd been coughing. I suddenly realized why I had been feeling so tired lately. It wasn't just that I was so busy.

Dr. Tom and the others told me I should check into the hospital at once. I protested. I was on my way to a special Holy Spirit Bible Conference in Augusta, Georgia. I was already packed and ready to go, and I didn't want to miss it.

Dr. Tom is a brilliant and learned man, but he didn't share my faith. Looking at the practicality of the situation, he didn't want me to leave his care, not even for a moment. But I knew that I was facing a big battle and I needed my BIG GOD TO HELP ME! I needed a miracle! I left for the conference.

Jesus said, "With men this is impossible, but with God all things are possible."

Matthew 19:26

4

My Stand of Faith

It's about a two-hour drive from the Atlanta area to Augusta, Georgia. The whole way I just thought and prayed about the morning's events. That night, during the evening service, the evangelist felt led by the Holy Spirit to pray a prayer specifically for people in the meetings who had cancer.

Yes! I jumped right up and ran down to the altar for prayer. My faith was so built up during those meetings! But in my hotel room I really had to fight fear. I watched that swollen lymph gland protrude further and further from the side of my neck. My body had betrayed me. Negative thoughts relentlessly bombarded my mind.

I started asking God question after question. The biggest question that weighed on my mind was one that might seem foolish to a lot of people: Should I receive treatment? You're probably thinking, *Well, duh, Pastor Mirek! Of course!*

But remember, my wife had been an oncology nurse for years. Living with her, I had heard stories of people who had taken chemotherapy treatments, suffered through terrible side effects, and died anyway. Sometimes they died not in spite of the treatments, but because of them! They left their loved ones saddled with thousands of dollars in medical bills. I didn't want that for my family, and besides, I truly believed that God could heal me without treatment. I wanted to be certain that I did what was best for me and that I followed God's will for me personally.

When I arrived back in Atlanta, the doctors performed a biopsy on that swollen lymph node. The official diagnosis was a form of lymphoma called Hodgkin's disease. Supposedly, in oncology circles, that was a good report. (I'd hate to see their version of bad news!)

My doctor informed me that there was a 60 percent chance that the treatment could handle this tumor, but he emphasized the severity of my condition. I was at the fourth and final stage of this disease, and he said that if I didn't start to receive treatment immediately, I would be dead within three months. I heard what he said, but I still had to kindly explain to him that I needed more time to seek God.

One of my favorite places to pray is in the picturesque mountains of North Carolina. I've often retreated there to wait on the Lord and seek guidance for major needs and decisions. This was definitely time for a retreat! I went to a rustic mountain cabin along the Nantahala River where I fasted, prayed, and sought God. I quoted and meditated on scriptures concerning healing, hour after hour, day after day. Faith began rising in my heart for a supernatural healing.

When I came home, I told the doctor I was still undecided on whether or not I should receive treatment. I wanted to wait awhile longer to be sure. Under great protest, he finally agreed. He had no choice, really. It was my life, my decision.

As the days wore on, my physical condition rapidly worsened. Sometimes at night I would wake up feeling my heart and lungs beginning to fail me. Linda started sleeping on the couch because the sound of my belabored breathing was too heart-wrenching for her. Although I knew where she stood, she never pressured me to have the treatments. She knew it was between me and God.

During those long, hard nights, we would cry out to God for help. Finally, relief would come and we'd thank God for His unfailing mercy. My life-and-death struggle intensified.

In my heart I just wanted to please God. I was standing in faith the best that I could, the only way I knew how. Throughout my life and ministry, I had learned to believe in His healing power alone for every ailment. Why should this time be different?

I knew the disease threatened my life, but was this healing going to be harder for God because it was cancer? Absolutely not! I didn't know it at the time, but I was about to learn some valuable life lessons.

"A man's pride will bring him low, but he who is of a humble spirit will obtain honor."

Proverbs 29:23 AMP

5

Renouncing Pride

When my dear friend and fellow pastor Bank Akinmola heard the news of my illness, he didn't hesitate. "We are coming to hold a prayer meeting at your church."

True to his word, the church came to pray. They brought a powerful preacher with them from Nigeria, Bishop Wale Oke. Bishop Oke is a great church statesman in his country. He holds large crusades and sees many people miraculously healed.

Together with our congregation, Pastor Akinmola's church prayed into the night, interceding for my healing. I was humbled and so grateful. I was grateful to God for providing a Body of believers to rally around me and grateful to the brothers and sisters who lifted me up in prayer.

After the meeting, Bishop Oke told me what he was sensing about my situation. I was surprised to hear what he had to say. He felt very strongly that I should receive the medical treatment while continuing to trust God. Now I look back at that time, it seems obvious. But when I was there in the moment, I was totally unsure. I so desperately wanted to believe God for healing and receive from Him supernaturally.

The Bishop shared the story with me about Hezekiah, the king who was sick and close to death.[4] At God's prompting, the prophet Isaiah had come and told King Hezekiah to get his house in order because he was about to die. Hezekiah wasn't ready to go. He cried out to God to deliver and heal him. The Bible says he wept bitterly for his life. God sent the prophet Isaiah back to the king to deliver a message that He would heal him and add fifteen years to his life.

Isaiah told the king what God had said and instructed him to place a lump of figs on his boil. A lump of figs! Hezekiah could have blown that off and ignored it. He could have said to himself, "Why would God need a lump of figs to heal me?" And he would have been right to a certain extent. Obviously, God can heal without any natural means. But if He instructs you to use natural means, it would be a good idea to obey Him! Hezekiah did and it saved his life.

There is a similar incident recorded in the Bible involving a man called Naaman.[5] He was looking to the prophet Elijah to heal him of leprosy. When Elijah told him to go dip seven times in the Jordan River, he became offended and refused to do it. In Naaman's defense, it was a pretty crazy thing to ask.

Did God need the river Jordan to heal a disease? Naaman certainly did not think so. He probably would have preferred a flash of light and an instant miracle! But God was only asking Naaman to obey a simple command. Naaman later repented, did the dunking, and was healed. Had he not obeyed, he would have gone home still a leper.

I continued to wait on the Lord, considering those scriptures, and digesting what the Bishop had told me. God began to speak to me about pride. Actually, He told me I was full of pride on the issue. I couldn't believe it! I was fighting the fight of faith and God was telling me that I was in pride? I argued with God. I did. I really argued with Him. I told Him I was standing in faith for my healing as I had learned to do over the years of walking with Him.

The Lord decided to show me in the Word what He meant. He led me to read in the Gospel of Mark where Jairus, a ruler of the synagogue, came to Jesus.[6] I had never seen this aspect of Jairus' story before, but the Lord made it clear to me. Jairus was a powerful man. He was one of the key leaders of the city. People knew who he was. But Jairus was desperate. His one and only daughter was dying. She was only about twelve years old and she was the apple of his eye.

When he ran to Jesus to ask Him to heal his daughter, he didn't wait and do it in secret. The crowds were all around, and Jesus was a controversial figure. Jairus threw all caution to the wind. He wasn't trying to approach Jesus as a dignitary; he was desperate to see his baby well again.

The Scriptures say that Jairus came to Jesus and **"fell at His feet."**[7] In his desperation, he abandoned his position, his status, and his pride. Before all of the people around Jesus, he prostrated himself on the dusty road. He humbled himself before God. He lay in the dust. He didn't care what people thought. All he cared about was the healing of his daughter.

The Lord showed me other examples of people humbling themselves before Him. Remember blind Bartimaeus? Bartimaeus sat along the roadside outside of the city of Jericho.[8] When he heard Jesus was walking by, Bartimaeus cried out loudly to Jesus for mercy: **"JESUS SON OF DAVID, HAVE MERCY ON ME!"**[9] Right in the middle of the street, he shouted at the top of his lungs. He wanted to see! People tried to shush him. They were probably embarrassed. Here Jesus had come to their town and some blind guy is screaming at Him.

Bartimaeus wanted to see. He wanted his healing so badly, there was no room for embarrassment. He cast aside his pride and became a desperate fool. He went right on crying out, **"Jesus, Son of David, have mercy on me!"**[10] To this day people call him "blind Bartimaeus." But Bartimaeus wasn't blind anymore! Because he was willing to humble himself before the Lord, Jesus was able to grant him sight. He's probably up in heaven right now saying, "Why don't y'all stop calling me blind Bartimaeus? I'm not blind anymore!"

The woman with the issue of blood exhibited that same humility. She risked everything by pressing through the crowds to Jesus. Because of her infirmity, she was considered "unclean." Yet she humbled herself, risking ridicule and abuse to receive her healing, and receive she did![11]

Again with the Syrophenician woman, we see a lady who humbled herself.[12] This lady had a daughter who was demon-possessed. When she pressed in to ask Jesus to deliver her daughter, He tested her heart. Jesus told her that it wasn't time yet for Him to heal the Gentiles and that He had been called to the house of Israel. He said, "It is not right to give the children's bread to the dogs."[13] "Dog" was a term the Israelites used to describe the Gentiles.

This lady could have really gotten indignant. "Dog? Who you callin' a dog?" But she didn't do that. If her pride had gotten in her way, she would never have received her miracle. But she humbled herself and replied, **"Yes, Lord, yet even the little dogs under the table eat from the children's crumbs."**[14] She stopped Jesus in His tracks. He praised her for having such great faith and said, **"For this saying go your way; the demon has gone out of your daughter."**[15]

The Lord used those stories to deal with me regarding pride. All that time that I had been refusing treatment, I thought I was standing in faith. But it turned out for me, it was pride. God showed me that I was more concerned with **how** I received my healing rather than the healing itself!

Many people of God have gone home to glory while refusing medical treatment, thinking they were standing in faith. They missed God's healing for them because they wouldn't humble themselves to receive on **another level.**

Still, I knew that I knew that faith in God's Word works. Jesus is the Healer. No one could talk me down from that fact. But I came to realize that my faith was not at the level at that time to receive what I needed from God. I had to admit it. I had to humble myself, get out of pride, and go to the doctor. That was a big step for me.

"A man's heart plans his way, but the Lord directs his steps."

Proverbs 16:9

6

It's Still a Work of Faith

"Let's go for it!" I said as I told the doctor my decision.

Upon my arrival at the clinic, I was ushered into the doctor's office. The drugs in the treatment he prescribed were among the most potent available. I was informed that they had powerful side effects, and even with the treatment there was no guarantee of success.

Going into this aggressive treatment was still a work of faith. I started to understand that I wasn't dealing with an either/or situation, but rather it was **both** medical treatment **and** faith in the healing power of God that would bring me back to health.

The doctor continued to gently and thoroughly explain what his patients usually go through. He encouraged me with the news that he had experienced a great deal of success in fighting my particular form of cancer.

I listened to everything the doctor had to say, but as he spoke something began to rise in me that said, "No, I'm not accepting these predictions."

I respectfully told the doctor that I believed I would have minimal side effects with the treatment and that I would not lose any of my hair. I sat there bold and confident in what I was saying. The doctor practically ignored me. He said that I'd better be prepared to buy a wig, because my hair was absolutely, positively going to come out. He had never seen anyone keep their hair while undergoing this kind of treatment.

I wasn't belligerent with him, because I truly respect doctors. I simply had grown really attached to this particular one as a friend. He had a warm and outgoing personality with a great bed-side manner. He informed me that he did not share my belief in God, so that made our interchanges especially interesting! But I wasn't going to let him shake my faith either.

"I believe it is God's will for me to keep my hair," I said. "The side effects I suffer will be minimal." I sensed God's assurance as I spoke. The doctor just gave me a slightly cocky, "We'll see" kind of smile. I began treatments within the week.

The first time I went in for a round of chemo, I was ushered into a large treatment room. There were about a dozen arm chairs there and that was pretty much the extent of it. I just sat there for a moment. Two nurses came into the room to check my vital signs. That wasn't so bad. Blood pressure cuff? No problem. Thermometer? I could totally handle that. It felt like any other checkup. When they had finished checking my vitals, they began to set up the treatment bags. They looked huge. Those gigantic bags were about to be emptied into my body intravenously for three hours.

"Can I pray over these bags?"

"Sure." The nurse looked a little startled as she slowly handed them over to me. "Is this going to be a long prayer?"

I couldn't help smiling. "No, it won't." I simply prayed for an effective treatment with minimal side effects.

During those first moments of treatment, as the chemicals slowly drained into my arm, I began to quietly praise God. I thanked Him for delivering me from this wretched cancer. Suddenly, I was overcome by the presence of the Lord. It was wonderful and truly supernatural. I sensed such joy and freedom in His presence that I began to laugh out loud. Apparently it was very loud because my wife, who happened to be on duty at that time, came over and told me to try to hold it down! I honestly did try, but "holy" laughter kept bubbling up out of me during the entire time of the treatment!

After about two hours of that first treatment, the nurse examined that swollen node on the side of my neck. It wasn't hard anymore. It was getting very soft and actually was shrinking while the first treatment was still running!

The doctor came into the room and I called him over to examine me. The node was now nearly gone! It was amazing. He said it was very unusual for anyone to see results so quickly. I really wanted my healing to be a testimony to the doctor. Over the long course of my treatment, we became good friends. Of course, I constantly told him about God's great love. I knew that God was going to complete my healing and I wanted the doc to see that God is alive and well.

I was serious about getting well. I cut off all extraneous activities and focused on one thing – my healing. I told my church members that I would preach and teach during services but would set aside many administrative duties. I would be resting and feeding my faith as much as possible.

My number one job was to stay on the planet to complete my God-given purpose on this earth. I decided to spend most of my time focusing on the Word of God like never before, especially where healing is concerned. I spent multiple hours with God reading the Word, quoting and meditating on healing verses. I read books on healing. I began holding weekly one-hour teachings on healing at church. The treatments continued month after month.

During my weekly visits to the clinic, I met other victims of cancer that I grew to care for deeply. Everyone had their own unique experiences, but we all were fighting to stay alive. It was a great opportunity to share the love of Jesus with people in these circumstances, especially when they knew I was right there in the trenches with them.

Sometimes my new friends didn't make it. I trust that the words I spoke into their lives took root and they are in heaven now. I particularly remember a young woman named Cathy who was fighting the same type of cancer I was. We sat in the same room and received the same treatment. One day she wasn't there and I missed her.

"Where's Cathy?" I asked the nurse. I could tell she didn't want to tell me, but she had no choice.

"Cathy had some complications set in. She died a few days ago."

I was in a life-and-death struggle. Again, that really hit me hard. It's so important that we let the world know that Jesus Christ came to bring life, healing, and eternity in heaven with Him!

While I was enduring the treatments and focusing on the Word, some dear friends of mine, Pastors Jeff and Patsy Perry, offered to send me to Rhema Healing School in Tulsa, Oklahoma. The school meets Monday through Friday, two sessions a day. The sessions are about two hours each, one in the morning and one in the afternoon. That was a pivotal week for me. I was able to just be alone with God and hear His Word on healing.

One of the teachers, Doug Jones, gave excellent teachings on the subject. He taught how God's power can be present without your physical senses being aware of it. Just because you don't feel it doesn't mean it's not there! He also said that faith in God's healing power keeps it at work in your body. You can't just give up on it. As I listened, my faith grew. I knew that I knew that God's healing power was at work in me.

The Rev. Doug Jones wasn't just a teacher. He was also the school's director and had been in that position for nearly nine years. I asked his opinion on my struggle between receiving medical treatment or simply standing in faith. He told me that he had seen thousands of cases through the years and his counsel was always the same. Every single person who attends Healing School is encouraged to receive whatever medical treatment is possible, and while receiving the treatments, come and also receive the power of God to heal through hearing the Word of God and the laying on of hands.

This may be obvious to you who are reading this, but many people struggle with this decision, not knowing when to receive medical help and when to stand only on the Word. The reality is: We need to do both. By the time I left Tulsa, I was greatly encouraged.

"The tongue of the wise promotes health."

Proverbs 12:18

7

Helps vs. Hindrances

I learned some valuable lessons during my fight back to health. One of the first battles I had to push through was the constant questioning of "why" this was happening to me.

Then and now, I truly believe that all sickness is from hell. Heaven has no sickness in it to send down to earth. If God is sending sickness and Jesus is healing it, then God would be fighting against Himself and it would be a house divided. But at the same time, it's only normal to ask "why?" when something like this happens. The key is to be sure that you're really looking for an answer, not just building bitterness in your heart.

If you're asking yourself "why?" in respect to the idea that you may have opened a door for the enemy to attack, that's healthy. But if you're shaking your fist toward heaven with a "Why, God, why?" attitude, then you can get yourself in trouble. When you're fighting for your life, you don't have time to get angry at the cosmos or ask the unanswerable questions. Seek God and get healed now.

As you do your healthy heart exploration, I believe that one of the first things to look for is underforgiveness. I searched my heart diligently and with much prayer. I wanted to be absolutely certain that I had forgiven anyone and everyone I might need to forgive or whom I may have offended. I sent letters and made telephone calls across the country and around the world. I really didn't feel that I was in any major unforgiveness, but I went ahead anyway just to be sure that I was totally clean. After all of the searching, I could not sense any one particular reason why I'd gotten sick. You may not find a specific reason either.

While you're searching your heart to see if there is a "why" in your life, be careful of listening to other people on the subject. Well-meaning people in the Body of Christ can unknowingly hinder people who are fighting terminal illnesses. Unfortunately, that happened to me repeatedly. Well-meaning brothers and sisters didn't hesitate to point out things in my life and personality that they perceived as flaws. They heaped condemnation and discouragement on me in the middle of the battle. I didn't need that.

If you know someone who is fighting death, don't try to discover the reasons why they might be in that position for them. Focus always on building that person's faith, offering encouragement, and doing your part to aid in their healing. Stay positive. If you truly sense there is an issue that needs to be dealt with, pray about it. God can reveal it to them and help them through it a lot better than you can!

If you're going through the battle yourself, you may have to make some tough decisions on what friends and family you allow to speak into your life. I had to make some sacrifices in order to keep my healing at priority number one, and you probably will too.

As the news of my condition began to spread, well-meaning friends would call me. I knew that they called out of loving concern, but the tone of their conversations belied the feelings of their hearts. I could tell that they weren't sure if I was going to make it. The doubt and unbelief in their voices started to pull me down and affect my stand of faith.

Because of that, I decided to no longer receive phone calls from anyone other than my very closest friends – people who believed that Jesus is the Healer and His resurrection power was at work in me.

Now, I realize that I may have offended some people by refusing to talk to them, but maintaining faith for my healing was more important than their fellowship. I spent my time reading and listening to God's Word regarding healing. I tried to avoid all extraneous events that did not add to my faith. I sought out meetings where the Word was being taught and God's power was present.

What I did was perhaps a little drastic, but for me it was necessary and it was scriptural. The Bible instructs us to **"keep your heart with all diligence, for out of it spring the issues** [or the forces] **of life."**[16] I sensed God directing me to guard my heart. That meant filling my heart with words of faith and thereby coming against the forces of fear, doubt, and unbelief.

One of my favorite scriptures is found in the book of Psalms, which says, **"He** [God] **sent His word and healed them, and delivered them from their destructions."**[17] I love that!

Here is a summation of healing truths that will aid in your healing, wholeness, and soundness:

- Spend time checking your heart before God regarding why you're in the situation you are in, but don't camp there. Move on.

- Actively search your heart for unforgiveness. Make every effort to forgive and release everyone you may have an offense against. Write letters, make phone calls, send e-mails, have face-to-face meetings – whatever it takes. Walk in love with everyone!

- Don't allow other people's doubt, fear, unbelief, and condemnation to pull you down. Stay away from all influences that don't add to your faith.

- Be sensitive to others with terminal cases. Be certain that you offer encouragement, faith, and strength in the midst of their struggle.

- Focus completely on your healing. Rearrange your schedule to reflect your number one priority. Stay on the planet so you can fulfill your God-given destiny!

"But if the Spirit of Him who raised Jesus from the dead dwells in you, He who raised Christ from the dead will also give life to your mortal bodies through His Spirit who dwells in you."

Romans 8:11

8

Encounters with God

"What's wrong with you?" the preacher asked. I was struck dumb as I stood before the man of God. I was literally, utterly struck dumb. I was totally unable to speak because of the incredible presence of God upon me. In fact, I wasn't even standing on my own because of the mighty presence of God upon me. Two men in the meeting were supporting me as Dr. Rodney Howard-Browne asked again, "What's wrong with you?"

What sounds I was able to utter came out only in the Spirit. As hard as I might try, I could not force English to escape my lips. Finally, my wonderful wife came to my rescue and I heard her explaining my condition.

Suddenly, the man of God laid his hand on my chest with great authority, cursed the cancer, and commanded it to leave my body. As he did that, I could literally feel fire shooting from his five fingertips. I distinctly felt spiritual fire leave his hand in five distinct streams of power. It was like being shot. There were five bullets of power shooting through my body. The force of it knocked me to the ground.

After that, I was totally lost in the glory and the presence of God. There was no pain in my body, only the incredible weighty presence of God. I wept as I lay there on the floor. It felt as though I was floating in oceans of liquid love. That's actually what it felt like, if you can imagine liquid love. I was weightless, completely enveloped and supported by it. I lay there for hours, totally oblivious to my physical surroundings.

As I started to come around, I awoke to see everything and everyone were gone! I was a guest at a pastor's luncheon when I got there, but by this time all the chairs and tables had been removed.

The only people left in that gym were me, lying prostrate on the floor, and the janitor! He was pushing one of those flat, four-foot dust mops in circles around and around me. I laid there watching him. I asked him why he was going around and around like that. He told me that he had been waiting for me to get up for a while so that he could finish dust mopping the last area of the floor. I told him that if he would kindly help me up, I would be more than happy to oblige. I stepped out of the gymnasium knowing that I'd had a divine encounter with God and I would never be the same again.

That encounter was part of a ten-day period that my wife and I spent in St. Louis in revival meetings with Dr. Rodney Howard-Browne. We went to all the meetings, both morning and evening, just soaking in God's holy presence and receiving His Word. When I left those meetings, my faith was built and strengthened and I was keenly aware of God's healing power alive in my body.

Encounters with God aren't always as dramatic as what I experienced in those meetings. Brother Hagin's Healing School was another time of wonderful divine encounters. Every morning and afternoon, I'd hear the Word of God on healing. Then I went back to the hotel to rest and reflect on what had been taught. That week truly helped position me to receive from heaven. The afternoon sessions were especially helpful because I learned so much in them. I was able to see familiar concepts in a totally new light. I encountered God by way of revelation.

The power of electricity has been around for centuries, yet it's been only recently that we have learned the laws that govern electricity and how to cooperate with them. When we work within the parameters of electrical principles, we get to enjoy the benefits! So it is with the power of God. God's power is available to free us from all sickness, yet we must learn the laws that govern the operation of God's healing power in order to benefit from them.

You can plug an appliance in, but if you don't turn it on there will be no power for it to work. Just because the power of God is present doesn't necessarily mean that you will know it is there, nor does it guarantee your healing.

The Gospel of Luke, in recounting what Jesus did to heal the sick, states, **"One day as he [Jesus] was teaching, Pharisees and teachers of the law, who had come from every village of Galilee and from Judea and Jerusalem, were sitting there. And the power of the Lord was present for him to heal the sick."**[18]

The Bible clearly says in this passage that **"the power of the Lord was present for him to heal the sick."** Yet the only one who received healing was a paralyzed man whose friends brought him to Jesus on a cot. The Pharisees received nothing, even though they were in the same meeting, hearing the same words.

When hands are laid on you for healing, **you must do your part.** You must believe that there is a divine transmission into your body. Then, you must constantly affirm with your mouth and believe in your heart that God's power is at work in your body. Affirm that God's resurrection power is actively working in your body restoring, rebuilding, and repairing all the damage that the sickness has caused.

That's what I did. I began to constantly affirm God's power at work in my body. I was coming into a new and fresh realization of God's truths on healing. In order for the power to be released, I had to keep my "faith switch" in the **"on"** position. I knew that if I spoke negatively or spoke against what God's Word states, then I would shut off the healing process. It's just like shutting off the light switch when you leave the room.

That truth became so real to me, especially since I was receiving chemotherapy. It's a great parallel. The chemo was injected into my body so it would work twenty-four hours a day, day after day. It was a continual process of killing off cancer cells. I couldn't see or feel it, but the effect was seen after many days. So too was the power of God at work in my body. I couldn't see or feel it, yet I knew it was at work, affecting a healing in me. If I hadn't positioned myself to receive by traveling to Tulsa and sitting under the incredibly anointed teaching, I would never have come to that powerful revelation. I went home praising God and keeping the faith switch on! I never looked back.

I experienced other encounters during meetings that other men and women of God held in our church. We invited Rev. Larry Hutton to minister on healing for several days. He was followed by revival evangelist Dr. Debbie Rich, who also flows strongly in God's healing power. There were many times that I was overcome by the tangible presence of God as I was personally taught the Word.

It's so important that we position ourselves to receive divine encounters. They don't all come from the pulpit. I received a lot just in my own time with God, reading books on healing and studying His Word. He ministered to my heart over and over again. Don't limit yourself! Position yourself to encounter God in church services, special services, meetings, crusades, Holy Spirit revivals, and prayer meetings. Go where the Word of God is being preached without compromise and where the Holy Spirit is allowed free course. You need to go to where the water flows. Don't die in the desert!

God *wants* to move on your behalf. He *wants* you to experience the joy of His yoke-destroying anointing that obliterates sin, sickness, and disease. Position yourself to partake! Too often people isolate themselves and go it alone, and it's to their own detriment. Thank God for the Body of Christ. Thank God for the gifts of the Spirit. Thank God for the ministry gifts in the Body of Christ. No man is an island. We all need help and we all need one another.

"Oh, give thanks to the Lord, for He is good! For His mercy endures forever."

Psalm 136:1

9

Discovering Mercy

As I progressed in the chemotherapy treatments, my body became extremely weak. As my faith was growing stronger and stronger, my body was becoming weaker and weaker. It got to the point where I could only concentrate on studying the Word for short periods of time. It was really tough to stay strong in faith in the midst of unending struggles, weakness, and fatigue. I was at the end of myself, but it was there at my own end that I discovered the mercy of God. When I had no more strength to stand up and fight the devil, I had to lean totally and completely on God's mercy.

There were many times when I couldn't stay alert long enough to prepare for my sermons. I was physically incapable of it. During those times, I threw myself on the mercy of God. The miracle of God's mercy came through each and every time.

Over and over again, I would stand up to minister the Word of God feeling completely tired, weak, and unprepared. As I cried out in my heart for God's mercy, the Holy Spirit would come upon me and I would sense His power and strength. As I opened my mouth to speak, revelation of His Word would flow out of me. I would walk off the platform after the service in amazement. When people complimented the message, I found myself saying, "That wasn't me. It was God!" If only they knew how true that was!

Trusting in God's mercy does not mean throwing away the fight of faith. It means embracing the realization that when you come to the end – the end of yourself, the end of your strength, the end of your abilities, even the end of your faith – you can throw yourself on God's rich and abundant mercy and find the help you need to put you over!

God's mercy is like the great ocean on which all the ships of God's spiritual gifts float. We receive a measure of faith to believe God through His mercy. We receive His Word, His gifts and callings, and His abilities all by His mercy. Mercy starts before faith and goes beyond it.

I had been taught well how to operate in faith, but the revelation of God's mercy was new and liberating! When I was not able to do the things I knew to do in faith, I committed myself to the mercy of God. In the areas where I felt like I wasn't measuring up, I trusted that God's mercy would cover it. I discovered that His mercy really does make up for our shortfalls.

When I began to tap into the revelation of God's mercy, I found His love so abundant and full that I came into a place of releasing everything to Him. I got to a place where I was no longer struggling for answers. I was just resting in Him, trusting Him to do what I could not. I learned to cry out for God's mercy and believe that it was mine every day. After all, without His mercy, where would we be? That realization will knock all the religious pride out of you! It's because of His great mercy that I am healed, not because of my great faith.

Just like the revelation of God's healing power flowing like electricity, I discovered that you can tap into God's mercy like an oil driller taps into oil. Oil drillers find the location of the oil (putting yourself in position to receive); then they build the structure to tap into the oil (receiving medical treatment, studying the Word, hearing a sermon, etc.); then they simply allow the oil to flow. When they've done all they can, the oil just continues to flow.

My testimony of healing is rooted in God's wonderful and abundant mercy. Had it been solely up to my faith, I probably would not have made it. We don't have to lie around and wistfully hope for God's mercy. The Bible says that we can come boldly to obtain mercy in the time of need! Mercy is something that we can obtain. It is a spiritual force that is available to meet the need of the hour when we're falling short. Thank God for His mercy!

"Keep yourselves in the love of God, look-ing for the mercy of our Lord Jesus Christ unto eternal life."

Jude 21

10

Lessons in Mercy

Vine's Expository Dictionary of New Testament Words defines "mercy" as an outward manifestation of pity and compassion. It assumes need on the part of him who receives it, and resources adequate to meet the need on the part of him who shows it.[19]

Mercy is more than a specific point of view, a feeling, or pity for the unfortunate. It assumes responsibility to act; to bring help, deliverance, healing, and whatever else is required to meet the need, even if the need is self-inflicted. Mercy isn't passive, it's active.

In the Old Testament, God instructed Moses to build a tabernacle, "a tent of meeting," where God could come and commune with man through the high priest. In the center of the tabernacle sat the Ark of the Covenant. The Ark was built of acacia wood, four feet long, a little over two feet wide, and two feet high. A lid was made to sit on top of the Ark that featured two winged cherubim facing each other. The entire Ark was overlaid with gold, inside and out. Inside the Ark, under that lid, were the Ten Commandments. God's Shekinah glory, His divine presence, appeared between the cherubim and above the Ark. God gave this meeting place a specific name – **the Mercy Seat.**

Moses received clear instructions from God and recorded them in the book of Exodus: **"You shall put the mercy seat on top of the ark, and in the ark you shall put the Testimony that I will give you. And there I will meet with you, and I will speak with you from above THE MERCY SEAT, from between the two cherubim. . . ."[20]**

God is simply saying that He will meet us where His mercy is. He meets us through His mercy and not through the requirements of the law. It is with mercy that He will cover our lack. Everything begins and ends with mercy.

What a wonderful type and shadow for us today. God visited man from the mercy seat, not the seat of judgment. One day He will meet man from the judgment seat, but right now He meets us with His mercy. The mercy seat covered the Commandments, signifying the atoning blood that was obtained from sacrificial animals. The mercy seat didn't nullify the Commandments, but it did supersede them and cover them. God's mercy covered man's sin, enabling God to fellowship with us. In the New Testament, the blood of Christ eradicates our sin, enabling His Spirit to indwell us completely.

Jesus taught the legalistic religious leaders of the day regarding mercy. As they took Jesus to task concerning His disciples eating plucked grain on the Sabbath, Jesus replied with a quote from Hosea: **"I desire mercy and not sacrifice. . . ."**[21] Religion calls for judgment and forgets about mercy.

Another time when Jesus was having dinner with the tax collectors, the Pharisees accused Him of fellowshipping with sinners. Again, Jesus answered them by saying, **"Go and learn what this means: 'I desire mercy and not sacrifice.'"**[22]

Jesus moved in God's mercy. He met people where they were and mercy flowed to them. Through His compassion, He was moved to heal the sick, cleanse the lepers, raise the dead, and yes, His mercy even spoke sternly to the Pharisees to break the religious shell in which they were trapped so they could be set free.

Throughout the Bible, the greatness and fullness of God's mercy is illuminated. The Psalmist declares, **"The Lord is merciful and gracious, slow to anger, and abounding in mercy."**[23] He goes on to say, **"The mercy of the Lord is from everlasting to everlasting** on those who fear Him, and His righteousness to His children's children."[24]

God has great mercy. It is without end. There is an abundant supply. There is never any lack of mercy for those who need it. King David said, **"I have trusted in Your mercy; my heart shall rejoice in Your salvation."**[25] This is the key: *to trust in God's mercy.*

The Psalmist also said, **"For as the heavens are high above the earth, so great is His mercy toward those who fear Him."**[26] I have always enjoyed flying. There is nothing like getting up to 30,000 or 40,000 feet above the earth and watching the world go by below. But even at 40,000 feet, you still haven't reached into the heavens. The height of the heavens is the height of God's mercy. Now, that's high! That's so high, it's a tough image to grasp! God our Father is trying to get across to us the vastness and the immensity of His great mercy. It is immeasurable!

In the book of Ephesians, the apostle Paul said, **"God, who is rich in mercy, because of His great love with which He loved us."**[27] Later in Timothy, he writes, **"For this reason I obtained mercy, that in me first Jesus Christ might show all longsuffering, as a pattern to those who are going to believe on Him for everlasting life."**[28]

In his early years, Paul had abused the Church of Jesus Christ, but God showed him mercy. God used Paul's extremes – going from a blasphemer and a persecutor of Christ to becoming the most outstanding church leader of his generation – to display just how vast His mercy is. God truly wanted to show for all eternity that it is through His mercy alone that we receive promotion and the blessings of heaven. Paul obtained great mercy.

In the second epistle to the Corinthians, Paul said that we serve **"the Father of mercies. . . ."**[29] Oh, what a joy to know that when the challenges of life arise to try to defeat us and when our faith seems at a low ebb, we can reach up and receive God's mercy to enable us to fight through to victory.

When I had done all to stand in faith believing and I was still standing, there were times when I sensed that I was beginning to lose my grip and the ground was dropping away from beneath me. It was especially during these times that the Father of all mercies came through with His compassion and acted on my behalf. In the arms of His mercy, I found strength and rest. As I waited and trusted in Him, His peace came.

Oh, I thank God for His great mercy. So great is His mercy that it is higher than the heavens are above the earth!

Throughout this difficult time in my life, God continued to speak to me about mercy. I learned to personally lean on and trust in His abundant mercy. My testimony of recovery is simply the greatness of God's mercy shown to me. When I reached ground zero in my emotions and in my physical capacity, I called on God's mercy. His mercy pulled me through. His mercy strengthened me. Mercy is obtainable! You just have to ask for it. God is generous – He'll give it to you!

Throughout my trial, I began to learn to tap into God's mercy. His mercy was there when I needed it most, even when I didn't seem to measure up. Great peace and rest came upon me as I learned to trust in the rich and abundant fullness of His mercy.

"*But thanks be to God, Who in Christ always leads us in triumph [as trophies of Christ's victory] and through us spreads and makes evident the fragrance of the knowledge of God everywhere.*"

2 Corinthians 2:14 AMP

11

Experiencing Supernatural Breakthrough

God's mercy is a supernatural force. It will pull you through any trial and keep you from going under! Remember blind Bartimaeus? He experienced God's mercy as he sat begging on that dusty road. When Bartimaeus cried out to Jesus, he did it because he had heard that Jesus healed the lame, the deaf, the dumb, and even the blind.

As he sat in his pitiful condition, his one cry to Jesus was the cry of a man who had nothing except a voice. He was a lowly beggar who probably felt condemned in his condition, without worth in the eyes of the religious leaders of the day. He knew he needed mercy since he had nothing to offer Jesus. He needed mercy because he had no social or economic standing. He needed mercy because he was an outcast.

Everyone told him to be quiet, but that only made him shout the louder: **"Jesus, Son of David, have mercy on me!"**[30] It was a cry to the very heart of God for His mercy. His cry of mercy brought him before Jesus. When Jesus asked what the man wanted, blind Bartimaeus cried out, **"Rabboni, that I may receive my sight!"**[31] Jesus said, **"Go your way; your faith has made you well."**[32] Immediately Bartimaeus received his sight. It was his faith that made him whole. Faith in what? Blind Bartimaeus had faith in God's mercy. He cried out for mercy and he received it!

Remember the Syrophenician woman? She also reached out for God's mercy. She came on behalf of her daughter who was miserably tormented by demons. She needed help and she was desperate. To the Jews this woman was an outcast, yet she boldly came to Jesus with a cry for mercy for her daughter. She knew she was not an Israelite, yet she would not be denied. See her determination. Hear the cry of her heart. She came up to Jesus, knelt down before Him, and began to worship Him. As she was worshipping Jesus, she continued to pray, *"Lord, help me. Help me."* Listen to her cry for mercy.

When Jesus told her, **"It is not good to take the children's bread and throw it to the little dogs,"**[33] He wasn't insulting her. He had legal reason for making that statement. Jesus was telling her that as a Gentile she had **no covenant right** to healing or deliverance at that time. His mission was first to the people of covenant, the nation of Israel.

This woman's persistence was admirable. She answered the Lord by saying, **"Yes, Lord, yet even the little dogs under the table eat from the children's crumbs."**[34]

This woman recognized that she was not a part of the Israeli nation. She was a stranger **"from the covenants of promise."**[35] She did not approach Jesus on the level of legalities or covenant rights, but on a much higher level – **the level of mercy!** Her continual pressing in for her daughter and her determination were based upon God's mercy alone. Her cry was one for mercy, and mercy she received!

Even people without a covenant with God have a right to His mercy. Jesus heard that woman's cry and He was truly impressed with her faith. The Lord Jesus Himself called her a woman of "GREAT FAITH." What an incredible honor! What brought her such great recognition from the Lord? What brought about total deliverance for her daughter? It was her undying, undeterred faith in the greatness of God's mercy. Faith that God's mercy was available to her brought her the healing that she sought. Everyone has a right to the mercy of God. Everyone!

Mercy is the underlying theme of the Bible. It's woven into the fabric of all Scripture. When Saul was doing his best to destroy David, David showed him mercy by not killing him when he had the opportunity. David had an understanding of the mercy of God. In fact, it was David who wrote, **"With the merciful You will show Yourself merciful. . . ."**[36] In order to receive mercy, you must show mercy. David received a lot of mercy in his life.

Jesus repeated this truth in the Sermon on the Mount when He said, **"Blessed are the merciful, for they shall obtain mercy."**[37] David needed mercy in his life for his sin with Bathsheba. When the prophet Nathan confronted David regarding his sin, David immediately went to God with a cry for mercy. He cried out, **"Have mercy upon me, O God, according to Your lovingkindness; according to the multitude of Your tender mercies, blot out my transgressions."**[38] David came to God not on the basis of the law, but on the basis of God's mercy. According to the law, David deserved to die for his sin, yet it was his cry for mercy that brought deliverance.

David's salvation came because he was quick to see his sin, quick to repent, and quick to call on God for mercy. The prophet Nathan told him that he was forgiven and that his life would be spared.[39] That's a wonderful example of God's mercy being extended to a man who reached out and obtained it.

When Jesus walked the earth, He embodied the mercy of God. He was God in the flesh, a God of righteousness, judgment, and truth; yet He came to show mercy to a world that was lost and completely devoid of mercy. He showed mercy to the thief Zacchaeus, thereby winning him to God. He extended mercy to the woman caught in the act of adultery. He extended mercy to the thief hanging beside Him on the cross.

Everywhere Jesus went He healed the sick, cast out devils, and raised the dead. He didn't do those things because of man's righteousness, but because of God's great mercy. Even when they spat on Him and hit Him with their fists, He extended His mercy toward all mankind. After they had beaten Him, pierced His hands and feet, and left Him hanging naked on the cross to die in the open, He prayed, **"Father, forgive them, for they do not know what they do."**[40] We deserved judgment, but God gave us mercy. **"Mercy triumphs over judgment."**[41] Thank God!

The well-being of our very lives is truly the result of God's mercy and not our own efforts. This concept is so totally liberating to me. It's because God is rich in mercy that we are redeemed from sin, death, hell, and the grave. It's because of His mercy. We need to revel in it. We need to love His mercy and come to have faith in the unfathomable height, depth, and breadth of His mercy.

The prophet Micah said it so well when he said, **"He has shown you, O man, what is good; and what does the Lord require of you but to do justly, to love mercy, and to walk humbly with your God."**[42]

When the pressure is so great that it seems your faith is coming up short, reach up and obtain God's mercy. Call on His mercy. His mercy will see you through. His mercy will meet your needs. When you pass through your battle and you stand in victory, it won't be a testimony of your great faith; rather, it will be a testimony of God's great mercy!

It's so easy to become like a Pharisee, basing our right standing with God on our right deeds. There's even a tendency to hold a "religious standard" on others around us, particularly those in the Body of Christ. If we're not careful, we can even get judgmental toward those who don't seem to be receiving healing or who have stumbled in their walk with God. It's when we stop showing mercy that we can become "religious."

Let's always remember that much mercy has been shown to us, and we need to extend much mercy to others.

"*Who are you, O great mountain [name your challenge]? Before Zerubbabel [insert your name here]* **you shall become a plain! And he shall bring forth the capstone** *[achievement — your healing and wholeness]* **with shouts of 'Grace, grace to it!'**"

12

Complete Recovery

As I continued to take my needed medical treatments, I also continued taking the Word of God, focusing on my healing. I went through chemo and radiation for nine grueling months. The treatments took a toll on my body physically, but spiritually I really saw the effects of taking in God's Word. Peace and rest in His mercy and love settled in on me. I knew I was in God's hands. The power of God was alive and active in my body, destroying harmful cells. I truly believe it was the process of being made whole.

Remember how I trusted God to keep my hair? It never did fall out! It was an outward, natural sign of God's mercy – a display of how much He really cares. My doctor was completely shocked. One time when he was examining me, he playfully tugged at my hair in disbelief. I explained to him – once again – that we serve a good God who is alive and well! He really is such a good God, isn't He? All of the side effects were minimal compared to what they could have been. I never missed teaching in a single church service throughout the whole time!

Finally, the day came when I was pronounced to be in full remission. In the medical world, once you have cancer, there is always the chance that it could return. They rarely regard you as healed or completely free forever, but the cancer is considered to be in remission. However, that's not so bad. They really ought to look up the word "remission." I did and I found good news! The root word for "remission" is remit. The definition of "remit" is to completely pardon, to cancel the debt completely. So I totally agree with that diagnosis: The cancer is completely eradicated and my body is clean and free of all cancer. And, it is never coming back!

Nahum the prophet said, **"Affliction will not rise up a second time."**[43] I confess that over my body continually. Today I am healed. I am well. I had to receive routine follow-up examinations for several years, but all traces of the tumor are totally gone. It's medically documented that I am delivered and set free from this disease. I give thanks to God for it.

It has been over ten years now and I enjoy perfect health. Since then, God has allowed my faith to grow exponentially. He has given me the grace and ability to build a church that touches the nations with the gospel of Jesus Christ. I am so grateful to be well. I am so grateful for my health. I am so grateful for His mercy. Oh, I thank Him daily! Because of His love for me, His great mercy reached down and helped me in my time of need. Today I am healed because of His power – the power I received from His hand of mercy!

"The earth, O Lord, is full of Your mercy. . . ."

Psalm 119:64

"Let Your mercy, O Lord, be upon us, just as we hope in You."

Psalm 33:22

13

God's Mercy, First and Last

For everyone going through a trial of faith, facing a life-and-death struggle, I write to you now: *What God did for me, He will do for you.* His Word is true and powerful. It will set you free. Reach out in faith now for God's mercy in your situation. Maybe you don't feel like you measure up in all your prayer and believing, but don't focus on that.

It is true that you need to do your part. Your part is to fill your heart with God's Word on healing. Your part is to believe God for His promises. Your part is to stand in faith on the promises of God and speak in agreement with His Word.

After you have done all you know to do, stand before God's throne and ask for His mercy. Obtain mercy for those areas where you may not be measuring up. Obtain mercy for your inconsistencies. Obtain mercy for your failings. Reach out and receive the mercy of God. Have faith in it. Trust in it. God will respond to your cry. He is the God of mercy, first and last.

Refuse the religious advice of those who would demean your faith. Refuse to listen to the devil's lies. Get with people who believe with you in God's healing power and who won't condemn you. Fill your mind with the wonderful promises of God's Word on healing and deliverance. Then, continue to press in, resting in His mercy.

My Prayer for You

I am concluding my testimony with a personal prayer just for you. Let's agree together:

Father, in the name of Jesus, I pray for the one who is experiencing adversities of sickness, disease, lack, or demonic oppression. Today may Your words encourage this person's spirit and mind and give fresh hope for healing, deliverance, provision, and total victory in their life.

Today we bind the power of the evil one to inflict hopelessness, defeat, condemnation, and fear. Go, in Jesus' name!

Father, right now we apply the blood of Jesus Christ to this mind, this heart, and this body. We speak freedom and deliverance from all doubt, fear, oppression, and negative thinking, and today we speak only words of life.

We confess that the resurrection power of Jesus Christ is released in this body, affecting a healing and a cure. The power of God is right now restoring, rebuilding, and repairing every cell to perfect health. Your power is being released to bring freedom of mind and spirit to receive Your miracle of total restoration.

We call on You today for Your rich and abundant mercy to make up the difference where we fall short. Thank You for Your mercy that enables us to rest in faith today!

Today we obtain mercy. Mercy from the throne of God. Mercy to meet the need. Mercy to walk in rest. Mercy to remain strong in faith. Thank You, Father, that today we receive mercy to meet the need in this hour. Thank You for victory, healing, and deliverance. In the mighty and strong name of Jesus Christ of Nazareth we pray. Amen.

RECEIVE GOD'S MERCY!

God's Promise for You

Do you feel far from God? Do you wonder how you could possibly get connected with the God who made this earth and you? How do I go about it? What is the true way to God?

The truth in the Bible is so wonderful! It says that God wants to embrace you, showing you mercy and great, great love. Everything that separates you from God has been eliminated. The things that put a barrier between you and God and that push you away from God are your own wrong thoughts and actions that go against what God declares to be right. The Bible calls these thoughts and actions "sin." Our sin pushes us away from God.

The wonderful and great news is, *God has erased the barrier of sin.* How did He do it? He did it by His greatest act of mercy ever shown to mankind. He did it by sending Jesus Christ to the earth as a man.

Jesus lived a sinless, spotless life, yet He took every human being's sin upon Himself on the cross over two thousand years ago. He paid the price of man's separation from God. So right now the door is completely wide open for every person on earth to receive the mercy of heaven.

So how do I receive? you are wondering. You simply admit that you need God. You must be honest enough to recognize that you've done things that have been wrong and that these things separate you from God. All you need to do now is to repent of your sin and receive the wonderful gift of mercy, Jesus Christ, by agreeing in your heart and saying the following:

God, I feel far from You, but I want to come to know You. I want You to be my God. I believe that I cannot get to You on my own. My sins have separated me from You. But Jesus, You gave

75

Your life blood to eradicate the sin barrier. Today I repent and turn away from my sins. I now receive Your gift of mercy, Lord. I receive You, Jesus, into my life. I receive Your gift of forgiveness. I receive Your gift of eternal life. Now because of my faith in You, I am no longer separated from you. I now have become a child of God.

As I invite You into my life, Jesus, take over my heart, my future, my ambitions, all that I am. I believe that as I take this act of faith that all my wrongdoings are erased. My sins are forgiven and forgotten and I now have peace with You and my Father God.

Thank You for filling me with Your love. Thank You for Your mercy. Thank You for calling me Your child forever.

I boldly declare that Jesus Christ is the Lord of my life, and I will love Him and serve Him forever!

If you have prayed this prayer, please contact us at www.worldharvestchurch.org. We are here for you. We will give you materials and whatever else you need to help you with your journey with God.

Endnotes

Chapter 2 – God's a Healer
[1] Acts 10:38 NIV
[2] Hebrews 13:8

Chapter 3 – The Surprise of My Life
[3] Jeremiah 20:9

Chapter 5 – Renouncing Pride
[4] 2 Kings 20
[5] 2 Kings 5
[6] Mark 5:22-24,35-43
[7] Mark 5:22
[8] Mark 10:46-52
[9] Mark 10:47
[10] Mark 10:48
[11] Mark 5:25-34
[12] Mark 7:26-30
[13] Mark 7:27 paraphrased
[14] Mark 7:28
[15] Mark 7:29

Chapter 7 – Helps vs. Hindrances
[16] Proverbs 4:23
[17] Psalm 107:20

Chapter 8 – Encounters with God
[18] Luke 5:17 NIV

Chapter 10 – Lessons in Mercy
[19] W. E. Vine, *An Expository Dictionary of New Testament Words* (Nashville, TN: Thomas Nelson, Publishers), 732.

[20] Exodus 25:21-22
[21] Hosea 6:6 & Matthew 12:7
[22] Matthew 9:13
[23] Psalm 103:8
[24] Psalm 103:17
[25] Psalm 13:5
[26] Psalm 103:11
[27] Ephesians 2:4
[28] 1 Timothy 1:16
[29] 2 Corinthians 1:3

Chapter 11 – Experiencing Supernatural Breakthrough
[30] Mark 10:47
[31] Mark 10:51
[32] Mark 10:52
[33] Mark 7:27
[34] Mark 7:28
[35] Ephesians 2:12
[36] 2 Samuel 22:26
[37] Matthew 5:7
[38] Psalm 51:1
[39] 2 Samuel 12:13
[40] Luke 23:34
[41] James 2:13
[42] Micah 6:8

Chapter 12 – Complete Recovery
[43] Nahum 1:9